Candy and the Tiger

Written by
Candice Restrick

Illustrated by
Emily Cramer

DEDICATION

To all the animals I've helped and to everyone who has listened to my adventures (especially my souley Josh).

Candy does not.

But one thing in common
and one thing they share
is a beautiful planet
which needs some care.

Now Fameye has never known a natural home.

His life is behind bars with no room to roam.

When they first met
it was love at first sight,
but upon seeing his cage
she thought,

"This is not right!"

She did her best
to always be near,
building a home
to give him some cheer.

The day finally came
when his new home was ready.
Candy opened the gate
but Fameye looked unsteady.

"Feel the grass under your paws
and go run about.
You deserve this and will love it.
I have no doubt!"

And with that Fameye ran from the cage to the trees,

enjoying his freedom with the greatest of ease!

"Farewell Fameye,
I'll be back one day.
I feel better now
knowing you'll have
room to play."

Fameye came back
and gave her a chuff,
which in tiger speak means,
"I can't thank you enough!"

Their stripes are not just on the fur, but on their skin too.

The tiger is the largest animal in the Felidae (cat) family.

Tigers are great swimmers!

Tigers can sleep more than 16 hours a day!

A 'chuff' is a greeting that tigers make by keeping their mouths closed and pushing air loudly through their nose. It's a bit like blowing air out from your bottom lip. Give it a try!

Tiger Quiz Time!

How many tigers are in the wild?
A) Under 1,000   B) 4,000-5,000
C) 6,000 to 8,000   D) Over 10,000
The answer is B, although 6,000 to 8,000 live in captivity. Tigers are considered endangered and some species have become extinct.

Bengal is the most common species of tiger. Can you name the others?

A group of tigers is called:
A) Ambush   B) Pride
C) Streak   D) Zippers
A or C. Tigers in the wild are usually solitary, but in captivity or with their young they are called a streak or ambush.

How You Can Help

1. Speak up for Wildlife: inform your family, friends and social media.
2. Recycle and Reuse: we all know how important it is for our planet and everyone in it.
3. Buy Responsibly: avoid products made with endangered animal parts or from things that will destroy their habitat.
4. Donate: various organizations can make a difference with your help.
5. Restore: plant a tree or clean up a beach. These little things can make a huge impact.
6. Volunteer: make a difference — even in your own community.
7. Educate: the more you know, the more you can help.
8. Pets: remember that wild animals do NOT make good pets.
9. Exploitation: never pay for exotic animal selfies or feeding experiences. This supports over breeding and poor living conditions for animals in captivity.
10. Food: wild animals were meant to hunt for their food. Never feed wild animals and put garbage securely away.

Follow the tigers Candice has worked with at Fortigers.org

Candice's bio:
After working with children for a gazillion years,
Candice decided to travel the world and volunteer with animals.
Yes indeed, it was with lions, tigers and bears...oh my!
Now she shares her experiences in a fun and informative way.

Emily's bio:
Emily works as a software developer and loves
to draw and play with animals in her spare time.
She especially loves her pet bunny rabbit and kitten!

Fameye's bio:
Fameye (pronounced "fam-eye") is a male Indo-Chinese tiger
from Thailand. He loves playing hide and seek as well as
finding interesting things to chew on!

Fameye in his new enclosure!

www.ingramcontent.com/pod-product-compliance
Lightning Source LLC
Chambersburg PA
CBHW040022130526
44590CB00036B/62